Ford's famous Dagenham assembly plant, where almost every British-built Cortina was manufactured.

The Ford Cortina

Graham Robson

A Shire book

Contents

ACKNOWLEDGEMENTS
All illustrations, including the cover, generously provided by the Ford Motor Company Ltd, are from the author's collection.

Cover: *The Cortina 2000E Mk III (1973).*

British Library Cataloguing in Publication Data: Robson, Graham. The Ford Cortina. - (A Shire book; 397) 1. Cortina automobile - History I. Title 629.2'222'09. ISBN 0 7478 0519 9.

Editorial Consultant: Michael E. Ware, former Director of the National Motor Museum, Beaulieu.

Published in 2002 by Shire Publications Ltd, Cromwell House, Church Street, Princes Risborough, Buckinghamshire HP27 9AA, UK. (Website: www.shirebooks.co.uk)

Printed in Great Britain by CIT Printing Services Ltd, Press Buildings, Merlins Bridge, Haverfordwest, Pembrokeshire SA61 1XF.

The original Cortina – 1962 to 1966

The Cortina changed the face of Ford – and of British motoring. In the 1950s medium-sized British cars had been heavy, old-fashioned and expensive. The original Cortina of 1962 was an innovation: it was hundreds of pounds lighter than expected, and much cheaper too. More than a million would be made in the first four years, and sales rarely slackened after that.

Before the Cortina Ford had had an unbalanced product range, but after its arrival there was something for everyone. When work started on the 'Archbishop' project in 1960 Ford-UK was making small Anglias, with 1 litre engines, and big Consuls and Zephyrs, but there was nothing in between. In 1962 the new Cortina not only filled that market gap but also offered a huge variety of models. By 1963, with the range fully developed, there would be 1.2 litre, 1.5 litre, 1.5 GT and twin-cam engined types, in two-door saloon, four-door saloon and estate-car derivatives. Here was a masterpiece of product planning, Ford-USA style, which squeezed every possible version out of one design.

There were two main influences behind its development. One was that Ford needed a new product to confront the BMC Mini, which was making all the headlines even though it was not making any money for BMC. The other was Ford-UK's quirky decision to compete, head-on, with Ford of Germany, which was currently developing its own new car, originally coded 'Cardinal' but soon to be named Taunus 12M.

In 1960 Sir Patrick Hennessy, Managing Director of Ford-UK, instructed his product planning chief, Terry Beckett, not only to surpass the Taunus but to create a new range of medium-sized cars that would increase sales, keep showrooms busy, make money and generally modernise the company's image.

Introduced in September 1962, the original Cortina was a front-engine/rear-drive car which had simple styling (and those now famous 'Ban the Bomb' tail-lamp clusters) and a rather stark level of interior trim and equipment. Powered by a simple,

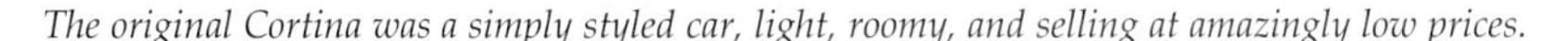

The original Cortina was a simply styled car, light, roomy, and selling at amazingly low prices.

In 1962 the cheapest Cortinas of all had a starkly trimmed front-end.

high-revving, 49 bhp 1.2 litre engine, it had an all-synchromesh gearbox (with steering column or central change), a beam rear axle, drum brakes all round and narrow tyres.

Even though the new car was almost aggressively simple (it would be another decade before Ford saw how it could make commercial sense out of a front-wheel-drive layout) the original Cortina broke new ground in two important ways. It was very light (aerospace body-shell stressing techniques helped) and it sold at astonishingly cheap prices. Conscious of what was unique to sell, Ford decided to advertise it as 'The Small Car with the Big Difference'. In other words, Ford's new car was larger and more capacious than rivals like the Morris Oxford and the Vauxhall Victor, but it was cheaper, delivered better performance and offered better fuel economy.

The Cortina was always intended to be built at Dagenham, the factory Ford had originally erected on the Essex marshes near the Thames.

Henry Ford II first saw the Cortina at a preview on the Montlhéry race track in France. He was enthusiastic.

The pundits, originally, scoffed at this approach because they were still dazzled by the front-wheel-drive layout and advanced suspension of the Mini (and BMC 1100) models. The public, however, never seemed to have any doubts. When they saw that a new Cortina 1200 cost a mere £639 (compared with £675 for a Morris 1100, and £702 for a Vauxhall Victor), there was a rush to buy. The fact that Ford could deliver from stock (while waiting lists still existed for some other models) helped enormously. Thousands of cars were built before announcement, deliveries began at once, and the Cortina jumped to the top of the list of bestsellers.

From the start there were 'Standard' and 'De Luxe' trim packs, along with two-door and four-door saloons, on offer. But there was more, for within months Terry Beckett's long-planned range expansion had begun. First came the better-trimmed 'Super', complete with a 60 bhp 1.5 litre engine, then automatic transmission became optional, and an estate-car type and the sporty 78 bhp Cortina GT saloon soon followed.

Even in 'Super' form, the original Cortina had a very simply equipped fascia panel. This would soon change.

The Cortina Super of 1963 came complete with better trim, and a 1.5 litre engine.

The real glamour followed during 1963 when Lotus, already famous for its racing cars, began building the two-door Lotus-Cortina, a saloon that not only used Lotus's own 105 bhp twin-cam engine but also had a new and more sophisticated rear suspension, and many light alloy panels. Meant for motor racing, the Lotus-Cortina soon became a sensation, though in road-going form it could be temperamental. To improve this, in 1965 the original coil-spring rear suspension was abandoned in favour of leaf springs and radius arms, which brought real reliability to a 110 mph car, though only about three thousand were ever sold.

Launching a car, 1962-style, with a sectioned example of the Cortina on stage to show off the technical features.

Early in 1963 Ford pulled off a publicity stunt when a Cortina Super was driven from London to Cape Town in record time. Such a journey would be politically impossible today.

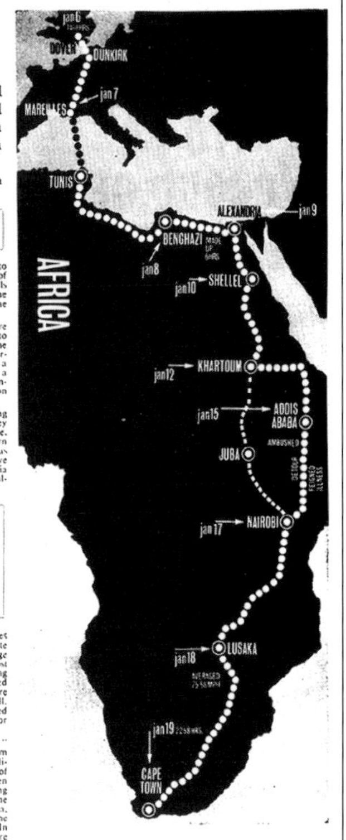

12,000 Miles in thirteen days

le reliability test a Consul er, Ford's latest model last week, was driven 12,000 miles from London 13 days.

ttention the car needed was a and light bulb!

From A. E. FABRIS

Jackson and Chambers had to find their way with the aid of petrol drums placed at intervals of three miles along part of the route and piles of stones on the tops of prominent hills.

For 300 miles the drivers were unable to use top gear due to the hazardous terrain. At one point their Cortina became airborne at 70 mph when it struck a sand-dune and nosedived into a gully, bending the front suspension which had to be repaired on the spot.

Due to this mis-hap, and being stuck several times in sand, they reached Khartoum 11 hours late, only to find that the southern route through the Sudan was impassable. The only alternative was to drive through Ethopia which added another 600 appalling miles to their journey.

IN THE NEXT BULLETIN
THE FULL STORY by Jackson & Chambers with pictures of their record drive

This took them 1,000 miles along a tortuous mountain route making it impossible to average more than 30 mph. The pair lost half a day through being continually stopped by armed police and other delays were caused by punctures—25 in all. Water had to be severely rationed as there were no supplies for hundreds of miles.

From Moggio the "road" virtually disappeared and from Neghelli to Moyale, where civilisation ends, the only means of navigation was by compass. When a band of armed men brandishing swords and spears ambushed the car south of Addis Ababa, Jackson jammed his foot on the accelerator and they scattered. In South Ethopia, conditions were

Below: *The Lotus-Cortina had a twin-overhead-camshaft Lotus engine and was intended for saloon-car racing. Here is the original car, posed at Brands Hatch.*

The Cortina GT, introduced in 1963, had 78 bhp, and a top speed of nearly 95 mph (153 km/h).

Right: *Advertised as Stirling Moss's 'Dream Car', this much modified Cortina appeared at the 1963 London Motor Show.*

Left: *For 1965 Ford facelifted the Cortina and introduced through-flow ventilation.*

After selling a quarter of a million cars in the first full year – all of them except the Lotus-Cortinas built at the Dagenham factory in Essex – Ford knew that its big gamble had started to pay off, though not even Terry Beckett could have seen that there would be Cortinas on sale for the next twenty years. A market leader when new, later versions of the Cortina would still be market leaders in the 1970s, and would still be respected cars in the early 1980s, before the Sierra project took over.

With through-flow ventilation, there were air outlets in the pillars alongside the rear window. What have always been known as its 'Ban the Bomb' tail lamps can be seen.

A 1965 model Cortina GT at speed. By the standards of the day this was a fast road car.

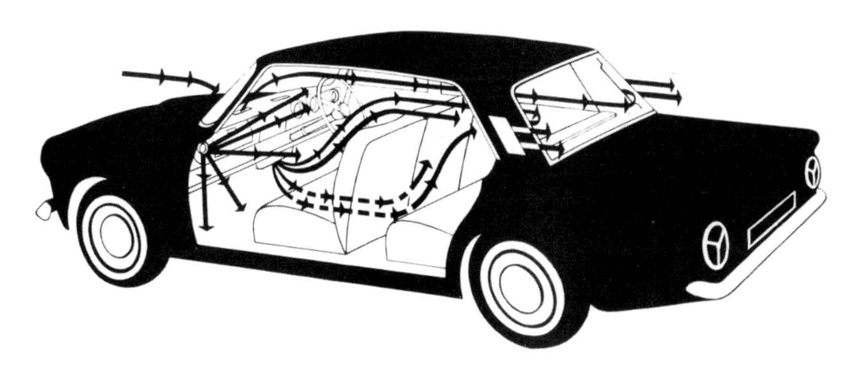

Ford's Aeroflow ventilation was a first for British family cars and was soon copied.

But Ford had no intention of sitting back complacently and introduced a series of improvements in the next few seasons. From late 1963 there was a new and more stylish fascia, while from late 1964 there was an external facelift as well as the introduction of yet another design of fascia and instrument panel, and the incorporation of face-level ventilation - a first for British family cars.

Even so, Ford never seemed to lose the thread of what the Cortina was all about - to offer value-for-money motoring to the motoring masses. By 1966, when the Mk I cars were in full maturity, the range encompassed twelve models, selling for between £648 and £1010. In addition, the Cortina had given rise to the pointed-nose Corsair, a

The 'Aeroflow' car's fascia was more completely equipped than before and had face-level 'eyeball' vents at each side.

Two generations – a Cortina Mk I passing the first of the new Mk IIs in 1966.

larger and more expensive car, which used a stretched version of the Cortina's chassis/platform and running gear, along with its own unique style.

By any standards, the original Cortina was a huge commercial and financial success, but after four years Ford was ready to replace it with a new and even better version. During the summer of 1966 the last of the 1,013,391 Mk Is was assembled - and a Mk II was on the way.

Cortina II - 1966 to 1970

Ford is, above all, a pragmatic organisation, so when the time came to replace the original Cortina, it moved cautiously, producing a thoroughly upgraded version of the original type. First with an entirely new body style and improved engines, and soon with new-generation engines too, the Mk II covered the same ground as the Mk I had always done - but with better fittings, more equipment, and an up-to-date look.

Announced in October 1966, the Cortina Mk II looked fresh, yet, hidden away where fashion was not important but function was everything, Ford had saved much money by retaining the original pressed-steel 'chassis' platform, suspensions and running gear.

Where the style of the original car had been craggy, that of the Cortina II was smooth - almost anonymous, in fact. Although each car rode on the same 98 inch (2489 mm) wheelbase and was 168 inches (4267 mm) long, the new car looked altogether larger and somehow more 'expensive'. The body shell was, indeed, 2.4 inches (61 mm) wider, as were the wheel tracks, this having been done to give a bit more elbow space in the cabin, but it was still a compact machine. No wonder, therefore, that the advertisement claimed: 'New Cortina is more Cortina.'

The marketing thrust of the new car was like that of the old: two-door and four-door saloons, plus an estate car, different trim levels, three different overhead-valve engines and (eventually) the super-sport twin-cam Lotus-Cortina model too. For the first model year the engines were merely improved versions of those already used in earlier Cortinas, the big difference being that the smallest was now to be a 54 bhp 1298 cc unit.

The latest car was, somehow, less blatantly mid-Atlantic than before (Ford-UK, after all, had an American parent). The original bench-type front seats and steering-column gear changes had been virtually eliminated, while the latest trim seemed more

Same platform, different style – a Cortina Mk II, as introduced in 1966.

The estate-car version of the Cortina Mk II was always very popular. This is one of the rare Cortina GT types.

'domestic', with carpets where the original version had used rubber mats, and with less bare painted metal in the cabin. For the first time, overseas manufacture began in 1967, at Ford's Amsterdam plant.

As before, changes and improvements were introduced regularly. Early in 1967 the Cortina GT (and, later, other Ford models) benefited from close-ratio gears, while the second-generation Lotus-Cortina (this time to be assembled by Ford at Dagenham, not by Lotus) arrived in March 1967. Then, in October 1967, Ford phased in the new

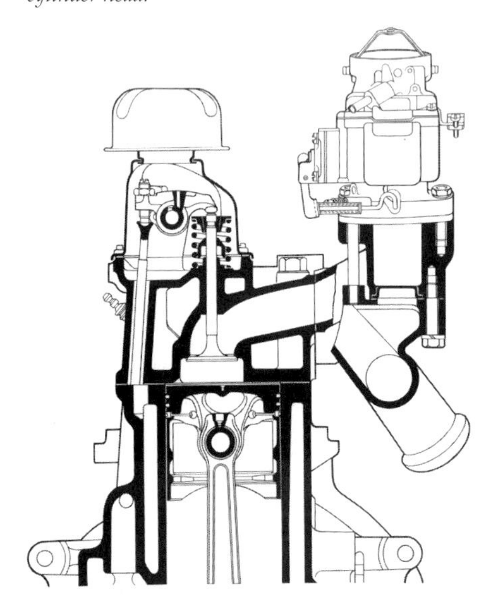

Up to 1967 the Cortina used an engine in which inlet and exhaust ports were on the same side of the cylinder head.

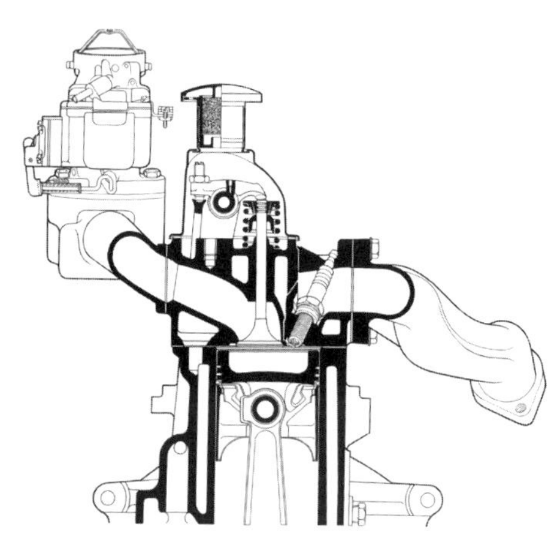

After 1967 a new type of 'cross-flow' cylinder head, much more efficient and potentially more powerful, took over.

Ford gradually moved the Cortina Mk II range up-market. This was the 1600E of 1967–70: lower, with stiffer suspension, than a GT, but with a luxurious interior.

range of overhead-valve Kent engines, which had cross-flow heads with bowl-in-piston combustion chambers, and which were more powerful than before. At the same time the mid-size Cortina engine moved up from 1.5 litres to 1.6 litres, with 71 bhp or (GT) 88 bhp.

At this time, though, the big marketing surprise was the launch of the Cortina 1600E, where E stood for 'Executive'. Here was a car that had cost mere petty cash to develop, but which was definitely a class above other Mk II Cortinas, and which because of its selling price (£982 at first) made Ford a great deal of money. In the next three years 55,833 four-door types and 2749 two-doors (these for export only) would be built.

Under the skin, the 1600E was pure Cortina GT, complete with 88 bhp 1599 cc engine, but the suspension was lowered and given Lotus-Cortina (stiffer) spring and

Cortina Mk IIs (this is a 1600E) shared the same slightly rounded style and were produced in two-door or four-door versions plus an estate-car derivative.

Although the 3 litre V6-engined Savage was a private-enterprise conversion by Race Proved, it gained limited support from Ford.

damper settings. Inside, the car was wall-to-wall luxury – plushy leather-look seat covers, thicker carpets, wooden fascia and door cappings, and an aluminium-spoked steering wheel – while outside there were unique Rostyle road wheels and special paint jobs to complete the makeover.

The customers (and the dealers, who found the 1600E easy to sell) loved it, for here was a new model with all the pizzazz of a Lotus-Cortina (*and* a set of wheels that no other Ford could use) but with a GT engine that was easy to service and maintain. It was a very appealing package, for there is no doubt that the 1600E handled better than its workaday relatives: when Cortinas eventually became 'classics', it was the 1600E that qualified first of all.

In the next three years, however, there was more to come for all Cortinas: the GT-type remote-control gear change was brought in on less-special versions, radial-ply

When England's football team defended the World Cup in 1970, every squad member was loaned a new Cortina 1600E for the summer.

The Mk II-shape Lotus-Cortina appeared in 1967 and was built until 1970.

tyres were gradually adopted, and reclining front seats also became available on all models.

Even though Ford had settled down to building its now customary quarter of a million Cortinas every year (and carried on disputing outright sales leadership in the United Kingdom with the Austin-Morris 1100 and 1300 cars), the product planners still thought there was scope for yet more improvements. Accordingly, from October 1968, a mid-term facelift was introduced, which saw the cars through for another two seasons. Although the planners considered it worth while, one had to look closely to see the differences. A new radiator grille, up front, appeared, while there was yet another version of the fascia layout inside. The bonnet release was now triggered from inside the car (making it easier to protect the car against theft), the much criticised 'umbrella handle' handbrake gave way to a proper pull-up lever, and there were new-style front seats.

Mechanically, the big changes were a new type of gearbox and change-speed mechanism, and a fully fused electrical system. Although it was not fundamentally changed, the Lotus-Cortina was officially renamed the 'Cortina Twin-Cam', though enthusiasts took absolutely no notice of this.

This was an impressive line-up, a range of fourteen different models, with four different engines, a choice of manual or automatic transmissions, and three body styles. Prices for 1969 started at £792 for a 1300 two-door De Luxe and peaked at £1163 for the Twin-Cam. (By this time the Race Proved company, led by the former racing driver Jeff Uren, had developed a private-venture version of the Cortina, the Savage, in which there was a 128 bhp 3 litre V6 Ford Zodiac engine; this gained approval from Ford, who supported it with a partial warranty, and it sold well.)

For the next two years these cars led Ford's sales efforts, but for the 1970s an entirely new type of Cortina was on the way. Between 1966 and 1970 a total of 1,024,869 Mk IIs (4032 of them Lotus-Cortinas) had been produced.

When Ford introduced the Mk III in 1970 it published this picture, which emphasises how far car styles (and female fashions) had changed in just eight years.

The third-generation Cortina – 1970 to 1976

After eight years, it was all change for the Cortina. Cars were getting bigger, Ford-UK was gradually moving closer to the centre of a new Ford of Europe concern, and families of new Ford engines and other 'building blocks' were all coming to fruition.

Then, as now, it was an almost immutable fact that cars got bigger, heavier and more expensive every time they were replaced, and this certainly happened with the third-generation Cortina. Conceived in 1967 (just as Ford of Europe was being founded), and launched in October 1970, this was a bigger, more ambitious, more 'transatlantic' Cortina than before.

For the first time, here was a Cortina that was developed in parallel with a new-generation Taunus from Ford of Germany. Although the two new cars had different outside styling (and in some cases stayed loyal to their own type of engines), they both had the same new-type pressed-steel chassis platforms, suspension layouts, and some inner body panels; they also shared a brand-new type of overhead-camshaft engine, the Pinto unit.

Except for some carryover engines and transmissions, the Cortina Mk III had little in common with the old Mk II. Although it was no longer than before (it *looked* longer, which speaks volumes for its styling), it was a more roomy car, with a 101.5 inch (2581 mm) wheelbase, and was 2.1 inches (53 mm) wider than the Cortina II had been. Unladen weights started at 2083 pounds (945 kg), still creditably light but not as outstandingly so as in 1962. In eight years Cortinas had put on 4.5 inches (114 mm) of width and were no less than 358 pounds (162 kg) heavier.

This time, too, there was no mistaking the Cortina III's transatlantic heritage. In many ways the shape, though smaller, was rather like that of the latest full-sized American Fords, complete with what became known as the 'Coke-bottle' bulge along

The Mk III-shape Cortina was larger, and had more sinuous lines, than the car it replaced. Most of the lines were influenced by Ford of America.

Top-of-the-line Mk III Cortinas had 98 bhp 2 litre engines, which made them useful as police cars.

the flanks, the full-width front grille (with four headlamps on some versions), and the very American-looking fascia and instrument display.

Its proportions, too, were different for, apart from the extra width and the more swoopy contours, it was a full 4 inches (100 mm) lower than the Mk II had been. The Mk III not only had to accord with what the Germans planned for their latest Taunus, but in the United Kingdom it also had to be a direct replacement for the Cortina II *and* the Corsair, which had died away in 1970 and would not be replaced.

For the specialist motoring writers, though, the interest was all in the new running gear. Not only was there the new overhead-cam Pinto power unit (with 98 bhp in 2 litre form) but also a new German-designed gearbox to go with it. Up front, this was the first Cortina to have a coil-spring/wishbone type of front suspension (previous Cortinas had used MacPherson struts), which was allied to rack-and-pinion steering,

From 1973 the Mk III was given a smart new fascia and instrument panel. The number of people buying automatic-transmission versions was growing.

but the rear axle was now to be suspended on coil springs and located by radius arms. Certainly this car handled and steered better than its predecessors, though in some cases at the expense of a hard ride.

As expected, there was a big range of Cortina IIIs – two-door, four-door and estate, 1.3, 1.6, 1.6 GT and 2 litre engines (but no Lotus-Cortina version, this vogue having

Above: *Like the earlier types, Cortina Mk IIIs were available in two-door or four-door form, plus an estate car, and in square-headlamp or circular-headlamp guise. Add in the various engine options, and the range was very large indeed.*

Left: *The Mk III Cortina had a wide and rather aggressive nose but was still remarkably light.*

Ford introduced the well-furnished 2000E for 1974: mechanically it was identical to other 2 litre Cortinas.

run its course), manual or automatic transmissions, and no fewer than five trim/equipment packs.

Compared with the old, here was a bigger, brasher, faster and better-equipped Cortina than ever: it had moved well away from its early-1960s roots. The bonus was that the 2 litre cars could now easily beat 100 mph (160 km/h), but the downside was that prices were up yet again - ranging from £914 for a 1.3 litre to £1338 for a 2 litre GXL saloon.

Right from the start, this time there were problems. Build quality was poor at first, and customers did not seem to like the rather flashy interiors, so it was perhaps a hidden relief for Ford-UK to suffer a long strike over pay in 1970–1, which gave time to improve the fit and finish of many parts before deliveries could begin again.

Sales, though, held up as well as ever, and in 1972 Ford produced 264,227 Mk IIIs for, along with the Escort, the Cortina was still one of the most popular cars in the United Kingdom, while it was also selling well overseas, particularly in markets like Australia and South Africa. Even so, the range became so impossibly complex that Ford eventually had to cut back on derivatives - getting rid of two-door GTs and GXLs, for instance - but in an average model year there would still be up to twenty different listed Cortinas.

In one fast-developing form or another, the Mk III (and its German counterpart, the Taunus TC) would be built until the summer of 1976, throughout a time hit hard by inflation, the first energy crisis of 1973–4, and industrial unrest. Yet in spite of the problems of building, scheduling and specifying all the cars, it was always popular, and always near the top of British sales charts.

The expected mid-life facelift (after all, British buyers were becoming more streetwise by the season) came in the autumn of 1973. Once again the car was moved subtly up-market and looked more desirable, for there was a smart new fascia and instrument panel, a tidier front grille, and altogether more 'British' trim and furnishing details. Also there were gearing revisions, changes to the suspension and a general tidying-up of specifications.

In addition, this was also the period when the 2000E was introduced, which proved an only partly successful attempt to match the old 1600E, this time with a Pinto 2 litre

Mk III estate cars were very roomy load carriers and sold in large numbers. This is a 1974 model.

engine. The wooden fascia, the seating and the furnishings were as good but, somehow, the character was deficient.

For the next three years Ford, like its rivals, fought to keep its prices down as much as possible, even though inflation was sometimes over 20 per cent in a year. There was little time for mechanical innovation, but for 1976 there was what was loudly trumpeted as a VFM (Value for Money) update, where each Cortina's specification was enhanced considerably – not before time, for the 1976 model 2000E was priced at £2456.

De-tuned 'Economy' models were introduced for 1976, but these were marketing flops and were soon discarded. The Mk III, in any case, was about to disappear, which it duly did in the summer of 1976, after no fewer than 1,126,559 cars of all types had been manufactured.

The final style – 1976 to 1982

By the time the fourth-generation Cortina appeared in the autumn of 1976, integration within Ford of Europe was complete. It was no surprise, therefore, to see that the latest German Taunus, which had been launched several months earlier, shared its style, and almost all of its engineering, with the Mk IV Cortina.

One reason for the delay, it seems, was that the new British Ford might have looked different from the Taunus, but a contrary decision was taken so late that the manufacturing of new body-press tools could not be completed in time. This was the last time that such individuality was even considered.

Though new on the outside, much of the engineering was like the Mk III under the skin. The entire chassis/platform of that car, the wheelbase (complete with its front and rear suspensions), steering, and general engine/transmission/axle layouts were all carried forward.

Only the new style, which was considerably more square and 'sharpened-up' than the old, was fresh and novel. The interior, subtly more spacious than before, even though the new car was only 2 inches (50 mm) longer overall, looked more like that of a Granada than an early-style Cortina and used the same smart fascia and instrument panel as the last facelifted Mk IIIs.

Even so, the two companies – British and German – still managed to hold on to some individuality as to which engines were used. For the time being every British Cortina used one or other of the well-known Kent (overhead valve) or Pinto (overhead camshaft) engines – from 50 bhp 1.3 litre to 98 bhp 2 litre, while the Germans went their own way by using similar engines plus two different sizes of overhead-valve V6.

The public, and Ford's own dealers, were delighted with what they saw for, as ever, they could pick and choose, mix and match, from the catalogues so that almost every individual customer could be satisfied. For 1977 not only were there two-door and four-door saloons plus estate cars, but there were also four different engines plus

The fourth-generation Cortina, the Mk IV, had much squarer lines than before, though it rode on the same basic platform as the Mk III.

Ghia versions of the Mk IV had a wood-trimmed instrument panel and very plush seating.

manual or automatic transmissions. Moreover, the later-famous Ghia badge, which had already been adopted on other Fords, was added to the line-up: this took the place of the E badge, which disappeared.

Although the glorious days when Ford built 250,000 Cortinas a year had passed (this was last achieved in 1972 and would not be resumed until 1979, and then only briefly), this was still a best-selling car by any standards. Every year Ford, as usual, was still sending between 30,000 and 40,000 kits overseas, for assembly in factories in Australia (where some cars had USA-type 4.1 litre six-cylinder engines) and South Africa, and now, with the Mk IV, manufacture also began closer to home, in Cork

Front and rear views of the basic Cortina shape, which Ford would build from 1976 to 1982.

Above: *Squared-up style, contoured 'sports' wheels and black trim around the windows all indicated that this was the sporty S version of the Mk IV Cortina.*

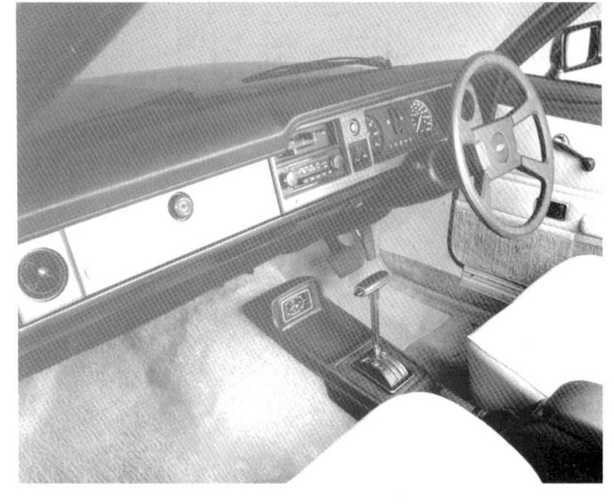

Right: *By 1976 standards, the Mk IV had a modern, well-laid-out fascia; the radio was standard (this was still a novelty for the mid 1970s), and there was a rev-counter on this Ghia version. The automatic transmission was an optional extra.*

By the late 1970s the Cortina had moved subtly up-market, being slightly larger, considerably more expensive and much better equipped than in 1962.

The first 2.3 litre Cortina was introduced in 1977, with a lightly tuned V6 engine giving effortless performance at the penalty of heavy fuel consumption.

(Ireland) and in Genk (Belgium), though the Amsterdam operation had closed down.

Even though inflation was raging in the United Kingdom, which meant that the cheapest 1.3 litre Mk IV cost £2045 (a 320 per cent rise in only fourteen years), the new cars were always seen as great value. Although Ford had long since abandoned the building of GT and Lotus high-performance types, right from the start with the Mk IV there was a firmly sprung S (for 'Sporting', we assume) type instead.

By 1977 Ford-UK's domestic market share was up to 30 per cent, a phenomenally high level achieved mainly because of sales conquests made over the hapless British

From 1977 the Cortina was joined by a larger, new-style Granada, which had very similar styling. In marketing terms this gave the Cortina's image a boost too. Then, for 1980, the Cortina was reskinned as the Mark V, though Ford officially called it the Cortina 80.

Although the Cortina Mk V of 1979–82 looked very similar to the Mk IV, almost every skin panel was different.

Leyland combine, so the company thought it could indulge itself a bit further. From the autumn a new 108 bhp 2.3 litre V6-engined version of the Cortina (this was the German type of V6, as already used in Granadas) was added to the range; there were several derivatives, with prices ranging from £3452 to £4795.

By this time the entire Cortina range comprised nineteen models, in three body styles, with four different engines and five trim/equipment packs. With prices starting at £2523 it was no wonder that the cars remained as popular as ever. The Cortina pedigree and theme were now fully developed and, when the pundits looked back at previous Ford practices, no doubt they started to expect another new style for the 1980s. But they were wrong. In recent years Ford had introduced more new models than ever (including already the first of the front-wheel-drive Fiestas and soon a front-wheel-drive Escort too) and could no longer move swiftly, or change as often.

Top of the range in 1980 was the Cortina Ghia. The name was from Ford's design subsidiary in Italy.

For 1980, therefore, Ford sprung a surprise. Previously this might have been seen as the expected facelifted version, but here was a much changed car. The company launched what it called 'Cortina 80' at first, but since everyone else (including the dealers, behind their hands) called it the 'Cortina Mk V', the official name was soon abandoned.

Not a new car by any means, nor simply a facelifted Mk IV, the Cortina 80 was a full and final restatement of a famous bloodline - and even at that moment Ford admitted that there would be no more traditional-type Cortinas in the future. The 1980s would offer much more wind-cheating styles, and a much more advanced chassis.

The Mk V (since that is what everyone else called it, we will use that name here also) still looked basically like the Mk IV and had the same proportions, but it was different in so many ways. Every skin panel had been changed and there was more window area; the roof was flatter while the front grille was wider and the tail lamps were hugely bigger.

Also, at the manufacturing stage an ambitious new rust-proofing process had been brought in, service intervals had stretched to 6000 miles (9656 km), there were new seats, a modified fascia, an 'S-Pack' suspension/wheels/tyres kit for most models (instead of a separate S model, that is) and a 'Heavy Duty' pack for some markets.

With more slightly different models than ever, with all engines retouched to liberate more power (now from 61 bhp 1.3 litre to 116 bhp 2.3 litre), and with saloon prices from £3346 to £5989, this was the marketing operation at which Ford was so adept.

Unsurprisingly, sales perked up again, to more than 200,000 a year, and in 1982 there was also the well-equipped Crusader special edition to attract the private owner. This time, though, time was catching up with the Cortina and, after 1,131,850

Compared with the Mk IV, the Mk V had larger headlamps, wrap-around front and rear indicator lamps and a subtly flattened roof panel.

Many of the final 1982 run of Cortinas were badged as Crusaders.

Mk IV/Mk V types had been produced, the last of 4,431,525 Cortinas was finally assembled at Dagenham on 22nd July 1982. There was time to look back, but not to go back, for the future lay with the Sierra, a very different car with all-independent suspension and a controversial body style.

Nothing could ever replace the Cortina, they said, and they were right. Ford still wishes that it will one day again produce such a trouble-free and universally popular family car.

The end of the road. The last Cortina of all was assembled at Dagenham in mid 1982. The managing director, Sam Toy (in dark business suit), was on hand to see that historic occasion.

Winners in motorsport

Although Terry Beckett had never considered the new Cortina as a competition car, Walter Hayes, a new recruit charged with transforming Ford's image on the high street, changed all that. Under Ford's new all-can-do banner of 'Total Performance' Hayes went about it in several ways. First, he encouraged the famous Lotus company to evolve, produce and finally race the Lotus-Cortina; second, he installed a dedicated motorsport department in new premises at Boreham (near Chelmsford); and, finally, he provided them with enough money to seek glory at the world's toughest rallies. If ever there was a way to convince the world that the Cortina was not a light car that was too delicate to perform on poor roads and at high speeds, this was it.

Although Ford enthusiasts usually know everything about the magnificent Escorts, whose exploits spanned more than thirty years, they often gloss over the 1960s, when the Cortinas laid all the foundations on which the Escorts could build. This was the decade when Lotus-Cortinas and Cortina GTs could not only win saloon-car races but beat the rest of the world in the East African Safari, when Formula 1 champions like Jim Clark could race Lotus-Cortinas (and even rally them, when they found time), and when the 'works' Cortinas were among the world's most successful rally cars.

Although the new Cortina GTs were successful in 1963 motor racing (that is, before Lotus-Cortinas), it was the Lotus-Cortina, with its twin-overhead-camshaft engine, that started to beat the once dominant Jaguars on the race tracks, just as Colin Chapman's little company intended.

Right from the start, in September 1963, the sophisticated two-door saloons were

When the Cortina GT won the East African Safari rally of 1964, the range was given an enormous boost. Peter Hughes (left) and Bill Young were the drivers.

winners, and it was not until later years, when a series of huge American Fords (Galaxies, Mustangs and Falcons) appeared, that they lost their winning ways. Not that Ford minded this development too much; it was happy as long as it was a Ford badge, whatever the car, crossing the line first.

Race-prepared Lotus-Cortinas had 150 bhp at first, and 180 bhp (with fuel injection and special preparation by BRM) by 1966, then from 1967, when the regulations allowed, they sometimes raced with ultra-special Ford-based 205 bhp Cosworth FVA power units. Even though the race cars could look ungainly on the track (early cars were noted for lifting their inside front wheels several inches into the air on corners, apparently without harming the handling one tiny bit), they were effective and, eventually, race-reliable for endurance races.

As power increased and handling improved, lap times tumbled - as did the opposition's fortunes. In Europe in 1964 the Alan Mann Racing cars (often driven by Sir John Whitmore) won six races and took second place five times in eleven starts, including the Brands Hatch six-hour Touring Car race. A year later the combination of Lotus-Cortina, Alan Mann and Whitmore won the European Championship outright, and very convincingly too. Sated with success, they never even tried to repeat that achievement.

In the United Kingdom, the 'works' Team Lotus cars were equally dominant. Jim Clark won the 1964 British Saloon Car Championship (three outright wins, five other class wins); the class-winning cars were totally successful in the years that followed and were still winning races outright after they had gone out of production.

Even the heavier Mk II car was competitive, especially when Frank Gardner drove Alan Mann's 205 bhp car in 1968. But then the even lighter Ford Escort Twin-Cam appeared and took over.

Lotus-badged cars were notoriously fragile in those days - the name Lotus was often interpreted as an acronym denoting 'Lots of Trouble, Usually Serious' - but against all the odds these cars were often successful in long events. Six-hour race

Using a Lotus-Cortina, which often cornered with a front wheel high in the air, Jim Clark easily won the British Saloon Car Championship of 1964, and he won many further races in 1965.

Before Jim Clark started the RAC International Rally of 1966, everyone thought it was a joke – but then he started setting the fastest stage times in this 'works' Lotus-Cortina. Jim, like the Lotus-Cortina, was very versatile.

victories became routine, while a Boreham 'works' car even finished fourth in the ten-day Tour de France of 1964.

Both types – Cortina GT and Lotus-Cortina – were successful in long-distance rallies in many parts of the world, though it was the simpler pushrod-engined GTs (whose leaf-spring rear suspension was more suited to loose going) that triumphed at first. Those were the days in which rallies were rough and demanding, and when unlimited service support was allowed: Ford developed specially prepared and rock-solid GTs with tank-like qualities and kept them going through all trials.

Although they were not very fast at first, Cortina GTs won two international podium places in 1963 (in which year the famous Pat Moss joined the 'works' team for a year, though she achieved little success), but there was more to come. In 1964 not only did Vic Elford and David Seigle-Morris win the Handicap category of the Tour de France, but Peter Hughes and Bill Young won the East African Safari, while Vic Elford was by far the best saloon-car driver on the French Alpine rally.

A year later the latest Lotus-Cortina had gained leaf-spring rear suspension and became a formidable rally car. Roger Clark won the Welsh Rally of 1965 (with the

Bengt Soderstrom and Gunnar Palm won the RAC International Rally of 1966 in this 'works' Lotus-Cortina.

Roger Clark, here seen winning the 1967 Scottish Rally, was one of the most successful rally drivers in a Lotus-Cortina.

author as his co-driver), and in 1966 Bengt Soderstrom not only won the Acropolis but also (by a country mile) Britain's RAC International Rally. That was the event in which Formula 1 champion Jim Clark competed – and crashed. 'You can't steer very well with the front wheels off the ground,' he quipped.

Nor should the four fine second places in 1966 be forgotten – Circuit of Ireland, Tulip, Acropolis and Czech. There was more success to come in 1967 – victory in the Swedish Rally for Soderstrom's Mk I, another win for Ove Anderson in a Mk II in the Gulf London marathon, and second overall in a Mk I for Vic 'Junior' Preston in the East African Safari.

In 1968 it was only the arrival of the new Ford Escort Twin-Cam that put an end to the Cortina's rallying success. Not only did the Escort use the same running gear as the Lotus-Cortina, but it was lighter, smaller, stronger, and it handled even better. With such a pedigree, how could it not succeed?

Only cruel luck, and a mechanical problem, stopped Roger Clark and Ove Anderson from winning the London–Sydney Marathon of 1968. Here they start the Australian leg from Perth.

Further reading

A number of books have been published on the subject of Ford cars, some of which contain details concerning the Ford Cortina. The following is a selection of those providing original material.

Burgess-Wise, David. *Complete Catalogue of Ford Cars in Britain*. Bay View Books, 1991.
Robson, Graham. *The Sporting Fords. Volume 1: Cortinas*. Motor Racing Publications, 1982 and 1989.
Robson, Graham. *Cortina: The Story of Ford's Best-Seller*. Veloce Publishing, 1998.
Robson, Graham. *Ford in Touring Car Racing*. Haynes Publishing Group, 2001.
Taylor, Mike. *Sporting Fords: Cortina to Cosworth*. Crowood Press, 1992.

Places to visit

Three notable motor museums and collections in the United Kingdom are listed below. None specialises in Ford Cortinas, but examples of one type or another are usually on show. Intending visitors are advised to find out the times of opening before making a special journey, and to check that Ford Cortinas are on display.

Haynes Motor Museum, Sparkford, near Yeovil, Somerset BA22 7LH. Telephone: 01963 440804. Website: www.haynesmotormuseum.co.uk

Heritage Motor Centre, Banbury Road, Gaydon, Warwickshire CV35 0BJ. Telephone: 01926 641188. Website: www.heritage.org.uk

National Motor Museum, John Montagu Building, Beaulieu, Brockenhurst, Hampshire SO42 7ZN. Telephone: 01590 612345. Website: www.beaulieu.co.uk